Reimagine HIGH VALUE SALES

Maa Saraswati

Reimagine HIGH VALUE SALES

SCIENCE & ART OF B2B SALES

Authored by

SHAKTI LEEKHA

Penman Books

Office No. 303, Kumar House Building,
D Block, Central Market, Opp PVR Cinema,
Prashant Vihar, Delhi 110085, India
Website: www.penmanbooks.com
Email: publish@penmanbooks.com

First Published by Penman Books 2020
Copyright © Shakti Leekha 2020
All Rights Reserved.

Title: Reimagine High Value Sales
Price: ₹699 | $9
ISBN: 978-93-89024-77-7

Dedicated

To

*All enthusiastic and honourable
sales professionals*

*Who sell goods, products or services
that benefit others*

To

All our customers & partners

*Who trusts us all enough to buy from
us again & again*

Praises for the Book

"I believe, B2B businesses are one of the most important and strongest pillars of nation building and would help in making India a global leader. Therefore, B2B marketing is evolving and is extremely critical for marketers as it makes them more creative, enhances their skills and increases their productivity."

—Mr. Amit Kumar,
A marketing specialist with over 25 years
of experience in the retail industry.
Senior Center Director at Phoenix market city

~ ~ ~

"This is a great primer for B2B sales. Shakti worked with me at UTC and I found him to be an astute, resilient and persuasive sales head. It is valuable to see his experience and insights documented in this book."

—Anand Stanley,
President & CEO Airbus India and South Asia

~ ~ ~

"The book covers India's journey in the last 2 decades, from liberalization to transformation. It provides business professionals with sales tools and strategies to handle various challenges, and last but not the least, it shares a road map for the nation, aspiring to become a 5 trillion USD economy."

—Prionka Ray,
Author, communication consultant &
psychotherapist. Founding Director, Sequel

~ ~ ~

"Reimagine High Value Sales" portrays the ground reality of B2B Sales with workable proven strategies to look at B2B with a different perspective. The author Shakti Leekha has a simple, lucid and conversational style of throwing light on one of the most complex subjects of our times."

—Mehernosh Randeria,
THE W3 COACH (Wealth, Wisdom, Wellness)

Preface

This Book encapsulates my professional journey *in marketing and sales space from the period* of 1990 to 2010, *when Indian markets were going through the transformations* in the form of liberalization; i.e. post-1991 era. This book shares the practical use of various strategies put in action in the ever-changing business landscaped post-liberalization which worked during the global meltdown in 2008 (Lehman brothers) and other events which left fortuitous impacts on our economy and people. This book talks about my journey and experiences in the last two decades while dealing with diverse people and the organisations in India as well as abroad. This journey is relevant to sales and marketing professional of all developing nations in the world. This, being my début writing work as a book and starts with a desire, to make meaning supposed to make money. Sharing my experiences to change the world of B2B selling by democratizing B2B selling education with simple and clear understanding. This is so critical for our nation-building and meeting our ambition of making Indian economy as

5 Trillion $ economy by 2025. A majority of exports are B2B sales either of core items like steel, cement, textiles, agricultural products & services, including software sales in an enterprise environment. By 2021 India will be the world's most significant construction and infrastructure market with a market size of $600 billion and the majority being B2B. For GDP growth, another big driver is start-up companies, which can grow fast in B2B as few large companies still rule the segment. Market is looking for innovation and the same can be done by innovative startups & finally, today ecosystem exists thanks to technology & platforms available now to interact with influencers and marketers which could help profit for B2B startup.

Market Metamorphosis, which is seen through my career, is presented in small stories; serves as food for thought for all people in related fields. This book will help all generations, i.e. baby boomers (born between 1946 and 1964) can relate with stories captured during there working life, Gen X (born from 1965 to 1979) will be part of this journey and also Gen Y(Millennials, were born between 1980 and 1994.), who are people who can understand how transition is taking place and this will help them better align and evolve with the fast-changing uncertain and ambiguous world now called the VUCA (Volatile, Uncertain, Complex, Ambiguous) world. Gen Z (born between 1995 to 2019), are heavy users of mobile, who was born with internet access, will see this book as history. This should empower and make readers more creative, enhance skills & increase Productivity. This legacy is created and will move forward in a journey with an aspiration of making India – Global Leader and Vishwa guru

The underline message for all is Mr Stephen Hawkins my guru's Quote "Intelligence is the ability to adapt to change" Intelligence is not experienced, and experience is learning over a period of time, which once shared is knowledge.

Acknowledgment

Thanks to many people who have made this book possible. Any time work such as this one is published, you can rest assured that more people than the author were seriously involved.

Firstly, I would like to thank my mentors, who have been a guiding light throughout my sales profession and have co-created some of the stories that I have mentioned in this book. Many of my colleagues and friends have supplied practical examples which has greatly enhanced the value of this book, and I am indebted to all of them.

Thanks to my family for bearing with me all these years while I was busy experimenting and living the stories that I have listed in this book. My publisher has played a key role in mentoring me in my debut book and guiding me at every step to create this knowledge sharing asset.

To those people whom I have unknowingly quoted or whose examples I have used without giving credit, I want you to know that we made every effort to find the original source. Though you are not mentioned by name, you are appreciated, and I want you to know that, as a fellow professional, I truly appreciate your contributions – Not only to the book but also the profession.

Foreword

Reimaging **High Value Sales** book is a scientific step by step strategy for all the Sales, Marketing personnel and Entrepreneururs to grow their business enormously!

Mr. Shakti Leekha has put all his successful practical experience in a Scientific and Artful way to grow your Business.

Shakti Leekha's simple style of writing offers a fascinating window into your mind and his scientific Blueprint will definitely help Sales personnel to grow and reshape their business.

His scientific and artful approach will help to overcome most of the obstacles and barriers in B2B sales, his action oriented approach will benefit to buil capabilities and exploit opportunities.

Wish you all the Best!

Dr. Ravi Kumeriya
Author of Amazon best seller book
"Design your Destiny"
Entrepreneur-Trainer-Life Coach

Contents

CHAPTER
One

*What's Selling & Uniqueness
in B2B Selling?*

Selling in most simplistic terms is the conversion of Product / Service / Ideas and ensuring exchange. This Exchange could be money or even batter trade. And sales being the most fundamental profession since the existence of mankind has been evolving and will continue to evolve with time.

Sales being a driver of success, in today's time, a seasonal Sales leader needs to achieve positive financial health for the organization and bring a positive change with limitation to budget and marketing expense.

Today one can achieve these results by using one of the following selling methods

1. B2B (business to business)

2. B2C (business to customer)

The approaches can be through

- Modern trade sales i.e. Malls and Retail format

- Direct Sale

- Multilevel Sales,

- E-commerce/Online/Digital

- OEM Sales

Approaches are essentially to answer the 'how' part of doing the sales, be it Physical presence in direct sales/ trade sales/Malls & Retail format or using Technology and doing as E-Commerce.

Multilevel sales is another way to reach customers, also known as network marketing. This can be both Physical, and Digital, i.e. enabled by technology.

B2B selling predominately comes in a play where the buyer and seller are both business entities. This is also known in many nations as Institutional Sales /Corporate/ Enterprise and in particular limited form as B2G (i.e. Business to Government sales). These form of selling is most complex and requires excellent skills along with compliance with the sales process. In this type of selling Executive Creditability is prime and it shall be dealt with in detail in other chapters.

B2C selling is business to consumer selling, in this type of selling the Brand awareness, Availability Reach & Price play essential roles. This selling process is like a well-oiled machine and becomes quite mature and once understood and can be replicated fast in organizations. There are many marketing gurus who have done herculean work on this and explained the process along.

B2B marketing uses the same principles as B2C; however, the only uniqueness is only in the way its been doctrine based on environment and precision of execution. Uniqueness in B2B can be explained with an example of a typical B2B sales, say selling any Building Capital Good or Solutions for Smart Buildings or Smart Infra.

The B2B industry is quite different from B2C, B2B is an environment wherein the sales cycle is large as purchase cycle is extended with multiple people being involved, the clients are looking at expertise, efficiency & emotional gain (Peace of Mind).In B2B environment selling the person selling is very critical as it's relationship-driven, and may give the feeling that decision is made on rational basis. Infact the reality is it's more emotional and is bagged by logic to justify. Business Value certain times can be some emotional /softer points of the person and political alignment more often as B2B sales person swing's deals by aligning and working on them.

B2B vs B2C Marketing

B2C Marketing	B2B Marketing
Product Driven	Relationship driven
Maximize the value of the transaction	Maximize the value of the relationship
Large target market	Small, focused target market
Single step buying process, shorter sales cycle	Multi-step buying process, longer sales cycle
Brand identity created through repetition and imagery	Brand identity created on personal relationship
Merchandising and point of purchase activities	Educational and awareness building activities
Emotional buying decision based on status, desire, or price	Rational buying decision based on business value

Source: http://masterful-marketing.com/marketing-b2b-vs-b2c/

STRATEGUS CONSULTING ©2015 Strategus Consulting

The marketing philosophy for all customer buying journey works on the AIDA model be B2B or B2C, in case of B2B AIDAS is a must beyond it AIDA, as further to action step if satisfaction is not derived then repeat business may not come and B2B relies more on account management to be sustainable.

The AIDA model is an acronym – it stands for attention, interest, desire and action. It is a model used in marketing that describes the steps a customer goes through in the process of purchasing a product or service.

Marketing activity is to create -Attention & Interest, promote – Desire, convert -Action and S is for Satisfaction further to action, which ensures repeat process to retain the customer and create delight.

THE OLD MARKETING FUNNEL

In B2B environment we always have a Client who is an Economic buyer, *who then has Influencers mostly internal*

in the organization or external in the form of Architect/ Designer / Technical / Engg consultant or a Project Management Consultant. Each of these influencer is a subject matter expert, and reviews/validates the proposal before the client takes any decision. The requirement documents are in some instances created by Influencers, which makes influencer role quite powerful as they set the question paper and evaluate too. Whereas buyer just funds the process and relies on the expert's opinion.

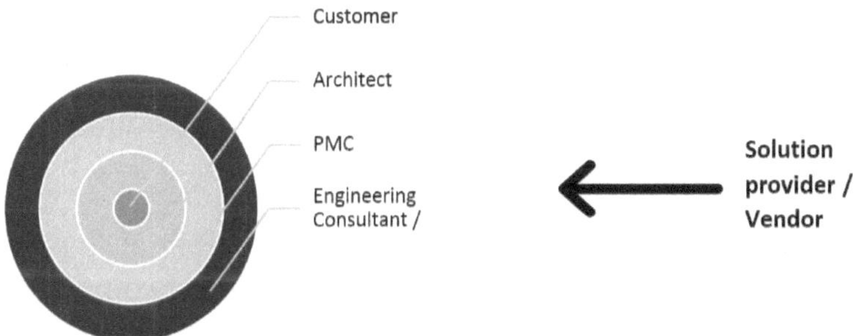

This makes B2B sales process quite complex, and a sale person flounders to reach the customer.

For example, selling a Vacuum Cleaner.

Apparently, most of us concur that selling a vacuum cleaner seems like B2C sales but involves all tactics of B2B sales and let's evaluate the steps involved. This relates to the period of 1990- early 2000's when still this selling was like a solution sales, now may be the model can be quite different, which is what is the journey of a Product from Concept to Commodity model. To classify this sale environment will be fit as B2C sale, which is a complex sale for the year 1990s.

Now as this is no more a concept /solution selling, its commodity and the buyer takes the decision fast enough for durables its total B2C sales since 2000 onwards and organisations running the durables model are classified as FMCD – Fast-moving consumer goods companies. They approach market both via B2B- Institutional Sales – Large High-Value sales & by Channels as B2C sales environment.

The Story in a period of the 1990s, Salesperson visits home meets the man in the house and gives a demo of the product, and the man invites his wife as well for the demo. After the demo salesperson understands that the couple is a working couple and ideal fit to be a qualified opportunity.

The Sales person, pushes his sales hard, trying to convince them. The couple then requests him to come back again after two days for a decision. When the salesperson visits again, he finds the maid opening the door, meets the couple and understand from them that the decision is not in his favour. After insisting on what's the gap or why such a decision is taken, he learns that user buyer, the maid was not taken into confidence, and she had raised objections and concerns on the offerings.

Initially, we realise in this method of selling, although it is B2C; still, it has a multiple complex matrices in decision chain, hence needs to be executed as B2B.

Similarly, even in Pharma/Life Sciences equipment sales where in patient will be a Consumer, though in the influence of a Doctor /Consultant who has prescribed the medicine and bought the same from a chemist who could have recommended some alternative as well based on the chemical formulation. The enclosed are part of Complex Sales process.

Many business books have defined Sales person Journey from being a Territory head to Area Sales Manager /Regional Sales Manager/National Sales Manager, & Mktg Heads or Business Heads. I have a different perspective and look at it not from designation or scope change, but the skill change aspect. This is very relevant in a B2B environment and rational way of progression.

There are Seven Levels of Sellers & Buyers Relationship:

Seller Skill Levels	*Buyer Types/Environment*
Teller	Commodity
Seller	Solution selling/Consultative
Hunter	Competitive/fighter pilots
Farmer	Repetitive/Account Management
Business Developer	Demand creation
Partner	Partner
Industry Network Consultant	Top-Down approach- Brand.

Teller uses "Spray & Pray" or show up and through up technique. The model is getting challenged and will be obsolete thanks to Digital/Catalog sales which will replace this type on selling.

Seller knows clients problems and is selling for needs and address Pain or Gain. The technique is the consultative approach.

Hunter is the fighter pilot of the sales world, who makes things happen! Ensures business keeps getting new customers.

Farmers manage an account and is known as key account management in specific markets.

Business Developer develops demand rather than reacting to a request.

Partner solves higher levels of problems of client's and follows the collaboration model. Business Partner helps the client to co-manage their business and takes the relationship from a Vendor to strategic vendor to a partner with at most trust and faith.

Industry Network Consultant is seen as an advisor & a resource by executives. The approach he follows is Top-down and is able to do so thanks to contacts built over the years throughout the industry.

The matrix of seller and buyer give rise to complex sales which we will explore in-depth in next chapter.

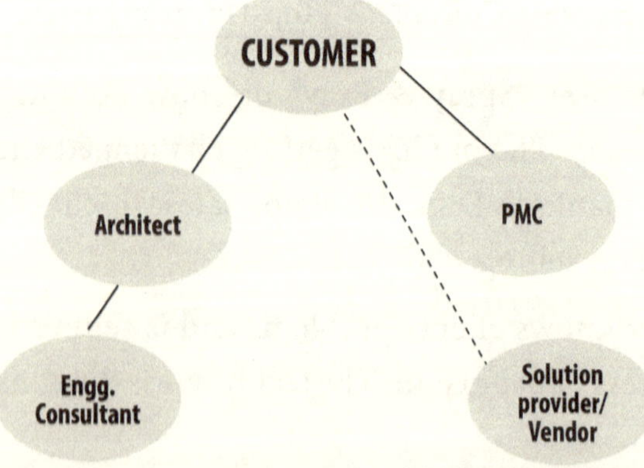

Approach each customer
with the idea of helping him
or her solve a problem or
achieve a goal, not of selling
a product or service.
– Brian Tracy –

CHAPTER
Two

What is Complex Sales?
Challenges, Solution-Sales
Process, Tools & Actions

Complex sale includes more than one decision-maker. Complex Sales exist in large B2B sales environment & in some smaller sales environment. This is commonly referred to as Enterprise Sales by some organizations.

In B2B sales the decision-maker is usually either the person who controls the relevant sphere of authority (predominantly, the CXO suite for technology sales) or the person in charge of all purchasing operations. Other interested parties might include the chief decision maker's assistant and gatekeeper, the product's intended users, the person or persons who will be responsible for setting up and maintaining the product, members of the company's legal team, and so on.

Complex sales of any type are further complicated by existing politics and power struggles within the decision-making team. For example, if you are selling to a husband and wife who have had an ongoing argument about what type of product to buy, their reactions to your sales pitch might be based on things they've discussed earlier and might be unexpected to you. Similarly, a company vice president engaged in a power struggle with the head of another department might either support or oppose the sale based on factors that have nothing to do with you.

The best way to make these internal struggles work for you is to get an advocate/Coach on the inside. Ideally, this advocate will be one of the decision-makers, but you can make do with someone who understands what makes the decision-makers tick (for example, a decision maker's assistant). An advocate can also clue you in as to who has the control of the purchasing process and who merely has influence. He can fill you in on the details of past sales and what issues will matter most to the decision-makers.

Often the ideal advocate is the gatekeeper. He is the one who controls access to the various decision-makers, so he can either make it easy or impossible for you to reach them directly. He also usually knows all the stakeholders as opposed to being familiar with just one department. Finally, the gatekeeper usually has the least to lose if your product doesn't work out, so he's probably more willing to take the risk of helping you than other decision-makers whose jobs might be on the line.

Another useful advocate in a complex sale is the person who has the most to gain from your product's particular benefits. For example, let's say that you're selling a cloud-based (meaning it's hosted online) software package that takes the place of traditional on-site software. A little questioning uncovers the fact that the CTO & CFO is over budget and trying to reduce spending as much as possible. You can then point out that your cloud-based system will save lots of money by eliminating the need for on-site maintenance and for hardware to host the package.

With luck, you can turn the CTO into your advocate, and you'll have an excellent chance of closing the sale.

Another major advantage in complex sales is being the first salesperson on the scene. If you are the one who initiates the buying process, you can frame the discussion in terms of your product's strengths. For example, if you sell a piece of equipment that's exceptionally reliable but not as fast as some of the other products in the market, you can stress the importance of reliability and cite figures about the costs associated with equipment failure in your presentation. When other salespeople make their presentations, the buying team will already be aware of the importance of reliability - and since your product is the best in this area, your competitors will look weak in comparison.

How does the ticket size /large deals close? The seven-step Sales Process.

A large ticket Sales can only be closed if we have a sales process. A sales process is which ensures and provides,

- A structured approach to selling

- Helps implement best practices

- Helps to focus the sales team to strategic plan and growth objectives

- Helps the sales team to provide the right solutions to right customers

- Results in better customer satisfaction

We have a Seven-Step Sales Process well proven with all types of B2B environment and Fortune 500 organizations in the world.

7 Steps of the sales process:

1. **Target**

2. **Qualify**

3. **Discover**

4. **Verify**

5. **Present**

6. **Close**

7. **Manage**

Step 1: Target

In this stage, we Prioritize Customer & Identify who are we selling, e.g., Owner, General Contractor, Consultant, Dealer, other examples which vertical market like Healthcare, Telecom, IT, BFSI & Pharma.

Step 2: Qualify

Qualify Buyer

Qualify Opportunity

At this stage of the process, we evaluate whether Company/Organization can provide solution to the target opportunity. We would also check the buying process of the customer to know the decision-makers,time frame for decision and the project progress with respect to plan/schedule

Step 3: Discover

Determine Goals

Determine Needs

Determine Risks

Determine Problems

At this stage we understand from the client the specific needs and challenges for the opportunity that we have qualified. We would also understand what they view as project risks and their criteria in evaluating the solution. This is the phase where we get to know how our solution might affect their business needs.

This would help us build the message of Value

Step 4: Verify

Verify Customer needs

Obtain Customer Commitment

At this stage, i.e. after the discovery step, we would reconfirm that what we have understood of customer needs is correct. It is essential that we have a positive response from the customer before we proceed further. This step helps to know the expectation of the customer and helps us to present our solution. It is essential to understand from the customer that he wants us to proceed further and sees value in our association with their organization.

Step 5: Present

Present Techno-Commercial proposal

Discuss and fine-tune the final offer

At this step, we present the solution ex: FAS quote,

Security system offer etc.

We also arrive at a mutually agreed value/delivery time to provide the solution.

Step 6: Close

Obtain Purchase Order

Acknowledge P.O

Organize Kick-off meetings

Prepare internal documents for transfer to delivery teams

Step 7: Manage

Build the relationship...

This is extremely important as we can be in touch with our customers to check their satisfaction with the ongoing works and to build relationships for future works and variations.

This is an important step that leads to account management which can result in increased business for the company/organization and repeat orders for other locations and other services that we offer.

In summary, the advantage of the seven-step process is the probability of Win is amplified by a factor of **3X** as :

Helps us to have better success

Helps us to sell the right solution

Helps us define the correct value message

(<u>to Customer</u>)

Provides **Value proposition**

(How customers values/view your solution as it affects their business needs/challenges and mitigates risk)

Differentiates from Competition

To ensure we understand the sales process as a science and manage it rightly, we have tools like Go-Get Analysis for us to understand better.

The tool helps sales leaders to make one -on- one more impactful, helps couching and gives a structure. Right culture and high success rate makes then a Winning team, which creates fast growing profitable enterprises.

			Go Get Analysis				
		Assessment Criteria	*Excellent (5)*	*Good (3)*	*Average (1)*	*Poor (0)*	*SCORE*
			Is there an opportunity?				
1		We are in touch with	Owner	Consultant / Architect	Main Contractor / Tender / RFP	Sub Contractor	5
2		Relationship with our contact from the prospect on this opportunity	Very close; Prospect is a loyal customer of XYZ products	Close; Prospect is familiar with XYZ products	Acquaintance; Prospect is aware of XYZ products	New contact; Prospect is not aware of XYZ products	5
3	KEY	Is there a compelling reason driving the customer to make a decision for this requirement.	Defined	NO RATING FOR THESE CELLS		Undefined	5
4		Is the prospect's business application of this project, objectives and the budgets clearly defined	Defined			Undefined	5
5		Is this requirement within our area of expertise and have we completed similar assignments earlier	Assignments of higher value in the same industry	Assignments of similar value in the same industry	Assignments of lower value but similar requirements; from the same industry	First such assignment in this industry/market segment	5

			Go Get Analysis				
		Assessment Criteria	*Excellent (5)*	*Good (3)*	*Average (1)*	*Poor (0)*	*SCORE*
				Is there an opportunity?			
				Can we compete?			
6		Can we clearly define the decision criteria/issues in order of priority	Defined	**NO RATING FOR THESE CELLS**		Undefined	5
7		Can we offer a solution to fit the prospect's compelling/driving reason	Yes			No	5
8	KEY	Rate the sales resource requirements to successfully close the sale with this prospect	Low			High	5
9		Have we defined the Unique Business Value and strategic benefits by which the prospect will prefer us as a business partner over other competition	Yes			No	5
10		Nature of the prospect enquiry / RFP / Tender	Supply based on BOQ	Design, Supply & Install based on BOQ	Design, Supply & Install based on the Lump sum	Only install and commission material supplied by the prospect	5

			Go Get Analysis				
		Assessment Criteria	Excellent (5)	Good (3)	Average (1)	Poor (0)	SCORE
			Is there an opportunity?				
			Can we win?				
11		Inside support	Prospect specified ABB products and has taken technical inputs	Have contacts to get more data on customer needs	Have the invitation to present Tyco Technical solution	Follow the specification requirement	5
12		How many competitors do we have on this prospect	We are the only bidder	Less than 2	less than 3	Greater than 3	5
13		ABB product composition in the solution offered	75% and above	Between 50% and 75%	Between 30% and 50%	Less than 30%	5
14	KEY	Have we contacted all the points where formal/informal inputs are given for taking a decision	User Buyer + Economic Buyer + Technical Buyer + Coach	**NO RATING FOR THESE CELLS**		Have we missed identifying even one of the 4 buyer types	5
15		Our relationship with the prospect on previous projects	Project executed ahead of time and client fully satisfied	**NEW PROS-PECT** or Project completed in time. Client satisfied	Project completed in time. Minor delay during commissioning	Project delayed. Client internal targets delayed	5

			Go Get Analysis				
		Assessment Criteria	*Excellent (5)*	*Good (3)*	*Average (1)*	*Poor (0)*	*SCORE*
		Is there an opportunity?					
Is it worth winning?							
16		The condition of the prospect's business	Rapidly growing with new expansion plans	Stable growth with few expansion plans	Minimal growth	Declared losses in revenue and earnings	5
17		Future revenue possibilities	The certainty of future projects and maintenance contracts	60% to 80% likelihood of future projects and maintenance contract on this one	30% to 60% likelihood of further projects	Less than 30% likelihood of additional projects	5
18		What gross margin will we be able to make on this requirement	40% and above	30% to 40%	25% to 30%	Less than 25%	5
19		Prior AR and Legal record of prospect	0 - 45 days	45 - 60 days	60 to 90 days	More than 120 days and/or Litigation	5
20		The strategic value and importance of this enquiry in terms of entry to new clientele, market segment, positioning, recurring business etc.	High	Medium	Low	**NO RATING FOR THIS CELL**	5
						TOTAL SCORE	100%

CHAPTER
Three

My Success Stories in B2B Environment

PROFESSIONAL SELLING AND CUSTOMER INTERFACE

Back in 1996, when I was part of an IT solution selling organization, the Internet wave has touched Indian shore. The CEO of a life sciences company contacted us. He wanted the convenience of having access to international markets at home 24/7 through the internet as it was inconvenient for him to communicate globally (due to difference in time zones) from his office during odd hours. Back in those days, having access to the Internet was a big deal and getting the required infrastructure was not easy. We took the opportunity to fulfil his requirement by providing him with the solutions available. The selling was outcome-based and not technology-based, and soon we understood that we needed to adjust to customer requirements.

Earlier, he had contacted bigger tech giants but finally bought from the people who gave him comfort and assurance. We realized after meeting him that corporate leaders are fast learners and have confidence in themselves; they are quite rigid on timelines and very specific and clear on their needs and requirements. He wanted to have good connectivity in evening hours to make international calls & conference calls. We went way beyond our duty, even went to his home multiple times to give live demos late evenings so that he gets the confidence in the solution that we were proposing. While dealing with such customers, the lesson learnt was that **people buy from people (size of an organization does not matter) and the executive credibility is the most critical parameter for taking a decision. Operational credibility/human element lies in gaining trust and confidence.**

This is how, in the real world, things move. In today's world, before buying anything or taking any service, we check for its reviews, ratings, etc.; which are nothing but experiences and credibility. **This is what is the Digital world.**

INSTITUTONAL SALES (COUNTRY'S LARGEST RETAIL CHANNEL)

This is a story which is critical for explaining the B2B (business to business) or institutional sales environment. This story is of the period of 1998 to the year 2000. We were discussing Canteen Stores Department (CSD) which at that point of time was one of the largest consumers for any FMCG or consumer durables company in the institutional market. This Department was created by the Government of India as an initiative way back in 1948, for providing a range of quality brands and branded products for defence personnel's and forces' daily use.

Any FMCG/FMCD environment where brand managers, marketers and salespeople are directly dealing with product and the dealers, with consumer demand, created sale mechanism which was straight and simple, compared to this requirement of canteen stores Department which is also known as institutional sales. This environment of CSD Sales is Complex Sales because the user interface is missing and the purchaser was quite different from the user.

Canteen stores in those days had various Area Depots where the material had to be billed and which was the hub for the CSD chain. The demand is generated from each unit run canteen and that demand comes to the area depot and the PO related generated from area depot office, the challenge which salesperson had was not on the product competing against its own category of product, but the product competing against the different category of products say a consumer durable against liquor, soap or suitcases.

Each unit run canteen added defined value or ticket size from which they used to put their demand note, thus, **the challenge for any sales person was to see that he gets the maximum share of product within that demand note.**

The Kargil Conflict happened in 1999, which was a huge disruption in demand cycle. Looking at the changed environment and thanks to close working and understanding of the Sales process I could create positive changes in the mix of the ordering pattern, thereby increasing the demand /sales of Audio systems like pocket radio sales & Tape recorders Cum Radio. This was done as our soldiers working in remote areas needed some entertainment and connectivity during this period.

Once in demand note, the share increased and the rotation worked; the success momentum continued. This is controlled Complex environment and each brand is trying to maximize its share. Today this is worth 3 Billion USD and is the largest Retail channel in India. Message for any business leader: **In every adversity lies an opportunity and we can tap only by being close to the Customer demand and understanding the complex sales process. Deeper insights are needed to unearth any solution.**

> **Don't find customers for your products, find products for your customers.**
>
> – Seth Godin –

INSTITUTIONAL SALES IN ONE OF THE LARGEST HOSPITALITY CHAINS

As we understand the B2B sales environment, executive credibility is critical for sale and beyond that in case of large, strategic, high value game changing selling environment, which is very complex, we need many more weapons to win. This story is about 8000 televisions to be sold to one of the India's largest hotel chains in late 1990's. The engagement started with the two teams seeing the demonstration of the televisions, gaining the confidence and giving the acceptance to the people behind the brand. This is the time when Koreans had entered the India market and Japanese, Korean and as well India brands were all in the fray. This complex sale was required to be cracked with the key decision maker, so that we have the top having comfort and eventually favouring the brand.

He was a hard task master , difficult to crack and was unapproachable. With the support of good office, we got him for a demo and engaged him in a conversation where we had topics of common interest. This helped us to walk an extra mile and get to an advantageous position building mind share with the top management.

This is the time when Indian televisions had moved from 10 channels to 90 channels. The challenge that the hospitality industry faced was, each guest had to tune the channels and each customer had to tune channels as per his preference. The hotel reception had to send a bell boy each time to help in tuning the channel. At this time the feature called "tuning lock" become very handy and we tactfully called it "hotel mode" feature. This helped us create a new range specific for Hotel with hotel mode feature.

The important learning is, as sales teams we have to go beyond customer acquisition mindset and look at creating value together with the customer as a partner who needs help in reducing his business pains & in turn create gain for his customers. Hence simple features like "tuning lock" gives operational benefits for hotel operations and create customer delight, as they now know in which channel what is being broadcasted & the program is locked.

The real reason of success in this large deal and largest hospitality deal of late 90's was adherence to the sales process and tool Go Get Analysis.

Refer to chapter 2 for the format of the go get analysis. Here , I will explain you how in this deal , the Go get analysis was used following the 4 steps , each having 5 quesitons. This also helps us in creating the 'winning' strategy for the opportunity. If you need more help with Go get analysis, pls refer to the link for the detailed tool and reach out for any further coaching.

Example of Go get analysis for the largest hospitality deal :

Step 1: Is there a opportunity?

If yes, then below mentioned five questions need to be answered:

Questions	Answers
Whom are you in touch with?	End User in this Case
Relationship with our contact from the prospect on this opportunity	Relationship is at OK levels

Questions	Answers
Is there a compelling reason driving the customer to make a decision for this requirement?	Brand uplift and Upgradation in Hotel. Well Defined
Is the prospect's business application of this project, objectives and the budgets clearly defined?	This is very well defined
Is this requirement within our area of expertise and have we completed similar assignments earlier?	This requirement within our area of expertise and have we completed similar assignments globally, would be India's largest and first of this scale.

At this stage, we understood that the opportunity is real.

Step 2: Can we compete?

Please refer the five questions for this step in chapter 2. The most difficult was to do discovery process and get to clearly defining the decision criteria, which in this case was brand reputation, serviceability and proven legacy of the brand. The compelling reason was quite apparent that the hospitality brand had now to compete against big global brands and wanted to come out as a leading brand with luxury positioning. Sales Resources needed were as well aligned, the Unique value that differentiated against all competition then was our brand of TV's being the legacy of innovation leadership and Trust. This value only helped us gain a position which was well aligned with client.

Step 3: Can We Win?

Win can only happen, if we have mapped all stakeholders in complex sales namely the User Buyer's, in this case, the General Managers of all the hotels, Technical Buyers the Chief Engg's of all hotels, Economic Buyers the C suite in the HQ's, the Corporate Procurement team, and coach, in this case, would have even the business development and executive support staff to various leaders who had been mapped so that the real team selling and value creation in solutioning and positioning is done.

Step 4: Is it worth winning?

This opportunity qualifies on the same as well, and eventually, once success was delivered, we turned and developed the customer as a managed account for the organisation.

In this case, **the learning was mindshare and positioning, can position us close to victory, but real Win only happens when is be backed up by positive customer experience and value (pain/gain) getting delivered with the solution.**

INSTITUTIONAL SALES IN ONE OF THE LARGEST BUSINESS GROUP OF INDIA YEAR 1999

One of India's largest business groups, Shakti, was growing and wanted to launch a new business line. They came up with an idea to launch an attractive scheme for signing up of new dealers with them. The scheme was, whoever signs up as a business dealer on the day of dealer partnership sign up event, would get a television for free. This became very lucrative, and the group expected 500+ partners to sign up on the day of the event. This generated a potential demand for 500+ TVs to be given away in the event. This order for 14 inch 500+ televisions was bagged by an organisation named Liptip, which had to supply TVs on the scheduled date on which the dealer sign-ups were planned by Shakti group. I as a salesperson working at Liptip had a challenge due to capacity constraint and the fact that 14-inch television manufacturing was not a priority item in the production schedule, as the margin realization for the Liptip was better for larger size screen televisions. I didn't want this opportunity in any case. Hence I went back to Shakti group and spoke to procurement leadership of shakti group & explained my challenges. I was very transparent with the client team and requested them to guide me through the challenges. However, the client wanted to cancel the order and go to an alternative vendor. The event was led by company owners themselves and by no means the procurement team could drop the call.

At this stage, thanks to the great relationship and professional credibility, we asked the client to suggest solutions for this problem. The client gave a solution; he asked us to keep the delivery truck and challan ready at the event site. The standing truck symbolized that incentives for dealers are aright there and lead to the successful signing up event. While the event went of, we at Liptip, had by now put the 14" 500+ nos, in our production plan. Shakti groups procurement team kept on guiding us on the next steps. We followed what our client advised and two days later, there was a list provided to us for the delivery of televisions, which now we could manage through our dealers in the trade locally. **Hence the learning out of this is, be open and transparent with the customers and customer will help & guide you as long as you are honest and transparent.**

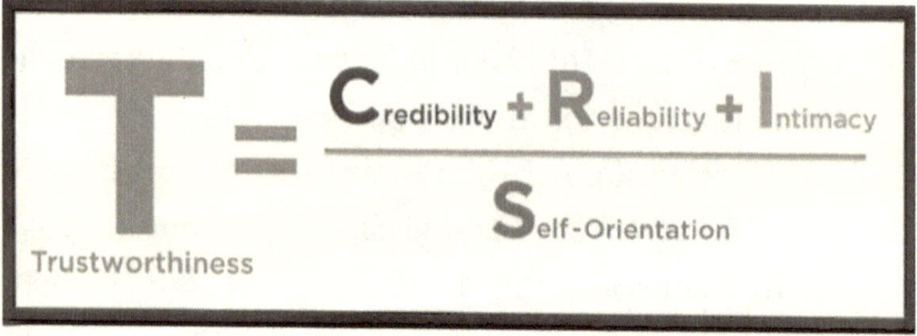

This case is a live example of treating people with respect, fairness & listening to them, which builds trust. The logic and actions demonstrate skills of influencing and establish one of the key secrets of the science of persuasion – Reciprocity.

Eventually, this crisis was turned into win-win for both brands Liptip and Shakti as now, Liptip channel could get 500 winners in there showroom's or dealer outlets for the Product, and they had the opportunity to upsell beyond the Prize. The advantage to shakti was that his business partners got a choice while at the showroom to pick the sign up award or buy sometime of more value with the additional gap being paid by the business partner of shakti. Beyond same the channel network of Liptip got 500 connects to manage and service at respective locations.

STORY OF ENGAGEMENT WITH ONE OF INDIA'S LARGEST FMCG GIANT

This story is of the month Oct-Nov, 1999. Diwali period had just got over, and an FMCG(fast-moving consumer goods) giant wanted to push more stocks in Dec/Jan months to distributors and business. This was because they had inputs, that in the upcoming budget, fuel prices are likely to go up, and as a result, transport strike may happen. Due to this, there might be a shortage of availability of goods with dealers. To counter the same, they wanted to get inventories built up in the chain to gain the market share and make the most of the opportunity. They simply wanted to push dealers to buy more stock. Hence, they wanted to plan a scheme for the partners. The FMCG introduced India's largest coupon scheme worth approximately one million USD. Pertaining to this scheme the particular dealer would get a coupon in exchange for buying more goods, they were excited as they could redeem those coupons for their own good and buy their aspirational consumer durable products. This ensured that the stocks were available while the forecasted strike happened and the company gained the planned growth in the market share, due to the availability advantages. The solution for the partner company was created via a Coupon redeem scheme for retailers so that they stock material for the period when we have transport strike. **Hence the learning is, to be successful we don't need just to manage self or the organisation but understand & predict environment & the dynamics and take advantage of the situation.**

STORY OF INTERACTION WITH A MOST POWERFUL INDIAN BRAND WHICH GAVE TOUGH FIGHT TO ALL MNCs

This story is of a beautiful summer day in 1999 when I was fortunate to be sitting with the leadership of a company A and working out trade schemes for them. I was in a meeting with the CMD of the company, Mr. X. He was sitting in a posh cabin with a whiteboard with crucial dashboards of crucial business parameters, a massive table above which was placed a calendar and four telephones — one each for internal communications, a board phone, other numbers and a direct landline. The direct landline was a red coloured phone with a push button.

Suddenly the phone rang and was immediately picked up. It seemed to someone really familiar and close on the other end of the phone. I observed him meticulously noting down names of specific points and junctions across the city, including Worli Naka,

Bandra signal, and Saki Naka. I had no clue what the conversation was all about but was I watching him carefully.

After completely noting down the list, Mr X exchanged courtesy with the person asking him about his whereabouts and his family; finally, the call ended with a very pleasant note. This call happened around 4 pm in the afternoon, and within minutes Mr X called the CEO of the company and told the CEO to dump the mango beverage stocks of the company with each & every retailer on all the locations that he had noted down, in the next 3 hours!! Ensuring that all the cash of the retailers are converted into the beverage stock of his company.

Next day I consciously thought what was so unique about those locations and I happened to pass by one of those locations, Worli Naka. To my surprise, I realized that the signboards at the junction carried advertisements of the mango beverage of A's competition brand B. This was the moment when I was able to comprehend the entire conversation Mr X had on the phone, a day before and how a successful business leader drives his business by being connected to the ground.

If you are still wondering what Mr X actually did, he got stocks filled up at all the key junctions where his competitor B was putting the advertisement. Brand B wasted huge sums of money, ensuring advertisements were put on key locations across the city. However no stock of the product of brand B was available in nearby retail shops and markets since they were already stocked with beverage of brand A on orders of Mr. X. This move proved to be very smart as during this hot sunny season people will feel like buying the beverage in the advertisement upon feeling thirsty; but since the nearby shops have the brand A's beverage stocked up, they will end up buying A's beverage and boost their sales.

Now let me tell you who was on the other end of the call. Mr.X had good relations with this one painter. This painter was responsible for the advertisements of brand B to be put up. Thus, Mr. X was well informed and was hence able to make the smart move.

Both had to compete, one to retain his share and other to gain but company A profited thanks to their dominant position and being lead by Mr X, a leader well connected to ground which is fortifying and creating all barriers for entry for brand B, which has spent on advertisement without getting the desired Return on Investment.

The learning from this episode is, being connected to the ground helps and getting all timely inputs, is required in order to be ahead in the game! Do whatever it takes to get the information first and have right connected for information flow which is fast, fair & furious.

In today's world, Digital Marketing, Social listening, artificial intelligence, algorithms, data processing & mathematical rules make organisations sense and evolve.

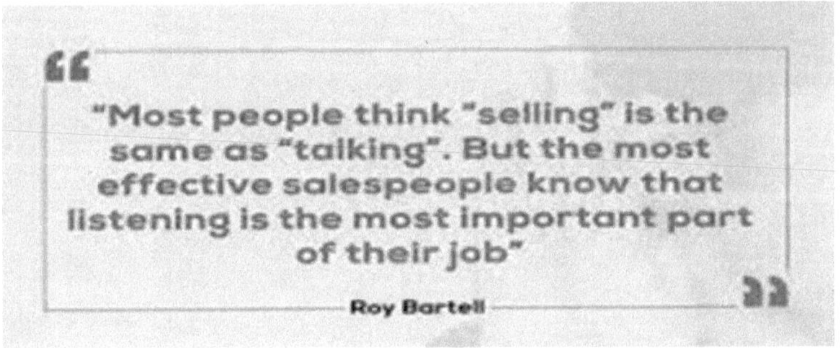

CHAPTER
Four

My Failures with Great Learnings in B2B & B2C Environment

This is the story of an era 1998 – 2000. At that time, we had planned a media advertisement campaign inside state transport buses for our televisions. We ran the campaign in more than 150 buses in a particular state. Unfortunately, the campaign was neither able to create the brand awareness nor increase the sales numbers. To review the progress of the campaign post 100 days of the launch, we called upon a meeting to discuss the progress and understand the reason for such a low impact.

Even after two hours of brainstorming, we were not able make any headway. Incidentally, at that moment we noticed a very senior business leader (who is currently board member in one of the top business house of India) passing by our conference room. We took this opportunity and invited him to review the ongoing campaign. After listening to us diligently, he asked us to re-create the environment of a bus in office, which was our site of action for the campaign. All of us struggled frantically as none of us had travelled in a state transport bus. We had appointed an agency to manage the campaign and we were just monitoring it remotely from our office.

I took the cue from the meeting, took a personal leave the next day and travelled by two state transport buses which were part of our campaign. To my surprise, I found that even during the day our advertisement was barely visible owing the colour scheme we had chosen. We all were looking at the creatives in our offices with bright lights (of 400 Lux and above) but in reality the light inside the state transport bus was not the same which made the difference.

We had an immense learning at that time that there are no short cuts, we must get our hands dirty by checking and validating things at the site rather than just conclude things from our office. **Nothing beats the validation at site in reality to create any campaign – imagine – check – pilot –check.**

Another failure during the same period was creating personalized Walkman with a Zodiac sign and colour. We had assumed that this personalization would create emotional connect and demand for the product. We also tried to position it as a valentine's gift. However we lost the game to roses which was tested and proven value for money formula.

We had an assumption that the looks and zodiac colour will connect with the youth and would help us increase our sales. However we realized later that people look for features and utility of the product. Moreover, our Rs. 1000 product could not stand and compete against Rs. 50 rose.

Millennials may not be able to connect with the above failure story and the product being discussed – Walkman has become obsolete and no longer exists as mobile phone has disrupted the entire industry.

As salesmen we lost many opportunities. We were seen as a product pusher rather than a solution provider.

Failure stories were always part of my quarterly review format, while being reviewed by the top leaders who mentored me during my initial career days.

Failures still happen and we really don't remember today and even track the same, so that learnings can be applied to ensure we don't fail in future for the very same mistakes or assumptions. With two above failures have clearly got my lessons and now always ensure test marketing is done. This reduces the probability of failure.

The lesson on specifically sales side is never take a customer or account for granted just because the relationship is going right for long numbers of years. We have to keep working and evolving with customer needs and in case the customer is in a challenged spot and we don't respond with care , and feel compliance . The trust and faith can get destroyed and competition who may better equipped to handle challenges takes the entry.

Have seen classic failure in such situations by complacent B2B account managers. We all have to be well aligned to market and client needs. Have failure example's where have seen organization's loosing big accounts with high profitability & value . This skill of empathy and evolving with clients and growing with their needs is very critical for a account manager, who needs make his organization understand clients changing pains and gain points, in a complex changing business environment.

CHAPTER
Five

New India Growth Engines

THE MUMBAI BKC REVOLUTION- BUILDINGS REVOLUTION -SMART

This story is of India's pride the BKC(Bandra Kurla Complex) – Commercial Capital's planned business district which came up post-liberalization as a world-class Infra as International Finance and Business Centre (IFBC) & creating Jobs for 0.5 Million people. While this area came with many Banking HQ bldg's as B2B salesperson then created various smart building solutions and delivered more than 18 Bldg's with our offering's. The leadership position established due to one global legacy of the brand, commitment of the organization and team alignment towards the market.

The learning's from experience in selling for HQ Bldg's to Malls, Airports and even data centres, which started coming up during same decade, the key learnings in each success has been as the Value /Deal Size goes up all deals start moving from Logical to Emotional parameters. This is true for all High-Value sales, in a mall the selling happened as could uncover that the owner wanted to communicate to pears he has arrived in business and wanted world-class solutions for Smart Bldgs. The competition was pitching him still on value sale, and we could Win as we understood the emotional need.

Hence with every passing day realization of strength of network and relationship kept on growing in my mind.

Trust me, after a point; we realize that 20/80 Pareto principle applies, the Mall ecosystem, Airport or any other Infra development we have the same 20% people involved who are influencing and have 80 % impact. Hence specifically in a B2B environment, we see a winning company quite distinct and ahead of its nearest competitor.

In case of an opportunity with an Airport to be inaugurated before committed global games deadlines, the selling from Top and creating the value of power and organizational commitment, helped us differentiate and close a deal over 50 M USD.

All large Infrastructure deals and complex sales in last two decades have been worked and Won with applied principles as shared in Chapter 2 and tools of complex selling with sales process implemented in the organization.

Trust me once done the success momentum ensures' s Winning is contagious, and the culture of the organization changes. As the company becomes a Wining company, the talent as well gets attracted, and the growth cycle keeps moving. This sometimes takes the B2B organization to the mode where the Winner Wins it all.

The message of value for all B2B sales leaders is a deeper understanding of Customer and usage of tools like "Go Get Analysis". We need to do opportunity assessment and planning, which mostly is answering a few questions with at most honesty and no assumption.

The few key fundamental are: Is there an Opportunity ? which can be only realized if we have the answer to

Compelling Reason, Business Objectives & Budgets defined or else this may not happen at all. The reason for change needs to be clearly understood if we say opportunity is there, as Status Co what is easy and loved by many. Resistance to change kills more than half of the opportunities. For a Salesperson, he needs to be the change agent and drive the change.

Can We compete? is another critical one to be answered in the form of Unique Business Value we bring or simplistic terms how we differentiate or position our solutions. More than 80% of Salespeople lose the battle at this stage as they miss the Discovery phase of the Sales process in their Seven step Journey.

Can we Win ? in this have we contacted all the points where formal/informal inputs are given for taking a decision. This is critical and engages salesperson to ensure mapping of all four key buyers: Technical, Commercial, User and to have a coach so that we can verify and validate as well with all and our coach. This step compliance is must and no solution presentation or demo to be done until this verification phase is completed. As jumping in the case be fatal in the war of sales. Certain times we may Win despite the mistakes done in process, but the same will ensure we leave profitability and certain time sustainability of the account on the table.

Is it worth Wining? This needs to be answered by the business before we get on to the War. As there is always a cost attached to working on a bid and if we don't evaluate opportunity rightly we may be focusing on the wrong one and could not be able to work on Qualified opportunities which can be Won, and we have answers to all questions and is worth Wining. This is more at Strategic level.

Success can be attained only by implementing and would request professionals to move from interest or intent level to committed level on adherence to the Sales Process and Deploy Sales Tools. Creating a Winning strategy with a Strategy driving tool is like a Science and will deliver 100% results. Move from just a B2B salesperson to a Resilient B2B Sales leader. Multiply and magnify massive Wins and Grow business.

The real growth heroes are the relationship builders, the business consultants, the sector experts and the growth engines for their customers. Sales Professionals take business strategy and make it happen; they take awareness & demand and turn into revenue. They seek opportunities and turn them into relationships that deliver benefits to all.

CHAPTER
Six

*Opportunities in Adversities
– 2008 Crisis-Recession*

The year 2008 triggered an era of the credit crunch. Lehman Brothers went bust, resulting in an economic consequence which had profound effect on global trade posting losses at a much faster rate as compared to a similar situation in 1930s. The economies globally slipped into a recession which in turn translated to mass unemployment.

Recession in general impacts both the economic and social phenomenon. Technically, 'recession' refers to two continuous quarters of negative economic growth. However, this narrow understanding fails to take account of the many myriad ways recession affects people's everyday lives. Recession for most people is a collection of experiences that may have a profound impact on their current and future well being.

Added to this global recession, India suffered the infamous 26/11 terror attacks in Mumbai.

The combined impact of these two crises crippled the Indian economy. FDI – Foreign Direct Investment dropped, real estate slumped and the investor confidence was shattered.

In the summer of 2008, just after the Lehman Brothers collapse, I was contacted by one of my previous employers. Since I had fond memories and regards for their management team, I accepted the invitation to the proposed meeting.

During the informal meeting with the Managing Director, the discussions focused on the current market scenario and challenges in India. Particularly interesting was the concept of Complex Sales and its differentiation when compared with consultative sales or upselling. We both agreed that surviving the recession could be done without downsizing the team as was the culture in US-based MNCs. It was important we decided, that in the short term downsizing might create a small bottom line positive impact on the P&L but would promote fear and affect the morale of the young team. Instead, if we were to train the sales team in identifying and managing complex sales, we would improve our ability to weather the recession. An offer to make this happen as the head of systems business was made to me, and it was a challenge I could not resist. I particularly liked the challenge because I was asked to take charge during the recession, and I was aware that this could be that life-changing opportunity.

Once I was on-board in late August 2008, the sales team and I scripted a sales execution strategy with SMART goals for our next financial year, which was to kick off from October 1, 2008. The team was aware that our overheads higher when compared to other players in this business. Also, with the emergence of other new players who were hungry for growth, our organisation had diluted its market share. There was also pressure on the profit margins since many players were now fighting for the market, which was limited in size owing to recession.

Our proposed plan of action for 100 days drafted by us which was focused on three pillars;

- Keep the morale of the team upbeat
- Believe that we are a Winning Team who will adhere to process with discipline and commitment
- Expand our basket of solutions to adjacent markets with enhanced skills

We embarked on our plan on 3 E's – Energy, Enhancement and Expansion because sustainable and profitable growth had to become imminent. Also, the four key values that the team embraced were the 4 C's –

Commitment

Consistency

Collaboration and

Care

Care was given its due importance as we were in a transformational journey. Tough times could break a few people in a team who needed support to get back to winning ways.

Complex sales is not a cowboy sales mission; it is about team selling. Complex Sales includes basic sales process and discipline, Business Development, Account management and inputs from project execution team to ensure better estimation and correct technical sales, customer goodwill, variations orders for additional works and repeat orders from existing customers. In this environment, word of mouth, appreciations, testimonials, referral plays a vital role to deliver the overall brand promise and retain plus acquire new customers.

The strategy was set, the play was on, and the mission to grow business in a sustainable and profitable manner was set in motion. His first action item was to bang on. The first success came from SEZs which were being set up in ORR – Revolution of the outer ring road and Whitefield in Bengaluru.

This was followed by the wins at India's largest Tech park in Chennai, commercial real estate growth in Lower Parel, Mumbai and Gurugram in NCR, Gachibowli in Hyderabad & Rajaghat and Salt Lake in Kolkata.

This momentum was massive and helped to increase the business backlog and grow our market share. Focus on creating key accounts among various MNC's and Indian businesses, making solid inroads and increase cross-selling of other companies of the organisation.

Dedicated account focus with key customers ensured repeat orders as trust was developed due to account teams pan-India. There was strong engagement with senior leadership of vendor and customer organisation wherein key issues were resolved due to speedy actions to enable win-win relationships.

The electronic Security segment too, has grown rapidly post 26/11 incidents. Protective Security 5 D's in action – Deter, Detect, Deny, Delay and Defend became name of the game. This was a huge change from the erstwhile

3G strategy of Gates, Guards & God. The government and private sector focused on three key areas of security- the physical infrastructure, the resilience of the security system and disaster management& recovery systems.

By 2010, technology had truly taken over. The internet became the backbone of systems in buildings to cover the aspects of comfort, safety and security. Innovators not only saw the opportunity inherent in connecting everything - but also laid the foundation to make these connections a reality through high-speed wireless, smartphones, and cloud infrastructure.

On reflection, crises of recession and dastardly 9/11 & 26/11 terror attacks in NY and Mumbai were converted into opportunities. On the technology side, In 2010, we were on the precipice of truly seeing what the internet could deliver, 10 years after the dot-com collapse and on the heels of the great recession, people were flocking to technology and away from the industries that let them down. Innovators not only saw the opportunity inherent in connecting everything - but also in the foundation to make these connections a reality through high-speed wireless, smartphones, and cloud infrastructure.

The crisis as an opportunity now, looking back, see that this decade has delivered the change starting from navigating the streets of unknown city, real-time traffic, shopping patterns have changed and Amazon as well creating a platform for meeting ever-rising customer expectations, thanks to Prime subscription.

This past decade delivered the changes from navigating the streets of unknown cities, real-time traffic alerts & management to shopping patterns. Customer expectations grew like never before, and organisations like ours were in the forefront anticipating and meeting/exceeding customer expectations.

Legacy or traditional players saw fierce competition from integrated digital upstarts, and it forced them to adapt to survive or simply perish. Many organisations embarked on long-term transformation. Innovations continued to grow, and above all these, customers gained at the end of the turmoil. Everything in life is work in progress, but the gap between customer expectations and vendor delivery has narrowed considerably.

This was indeed opportunity for organizations who had robust sales processes and B2B strategy, strong business solutions and a robust delivery system to survive the onslaught of the external environment. This is the time when organisations survived and grew due to good management, quality solutions from sales to execution and beyond, excellent teams and the skill and will to grow in tough times in a resolute manner.

As in low tides, we get to know who swimming nude is and exposes the resilience of an organization. This is the time when tough sales guys survive, and the organizations flourish who have the right people, process or skill and will to make most of the tough times. Its also the times which teach many sales, marketing and business professionals to realize that B2B large value selling is more from "We" not "I" mode which leads to illness not Wellness. The same word illness if you replace with we change the world for all.

CHAPTER
Seven

FDI & Acquisitions in India

FDI - Foreign direct investment includes "mergers and acquisitions, building new facilities, reinvesting profits earned from overseas operations, and intra company loans". In a narrow sense, foreign direct investment refers just to building new facility, and a lasting management interest (10 % or more of voting stock) in an enterprise operating in an economy other than that of the investor. FDI is the sum of equity capital, long-term capital, and short-term capital, as shown in the balance of payments. FDI usually involves participation in management, joint venture, transfer of technology and expertise.

During the last two decades, we saw FDI worth close to 400 $ Billion flowing in across all industries and sectors in all forms, either equity or full ownerships. This as well transformed the nation with not just investment but also brought along various global practices of business. In this scenario, I have two stories to share where in FDI came in India for the acquisition of local Indian companies and impact of same.

One relates to the period of late 1999 – 2004, in which one global fortune 500 player invested in the sunrise sector company in India by acquiring regional leaders, thereby creating national presence for the Global Organisation. This has been a Success though the challenges were many, while this journey embarked, starting from Cultural to managerial styles as well. The sales approach at one time was to manage Sales in B2B environment rather than Professional selling as the market was not that big and players few. However, the MNC's (Multinational Company) that came in had FCPA compliance and other global compliances, and so they wanted a structured approach to selling or what is known as Professional Selling. Hence after acquisition, this approach turned into a cultural as well as technical challenge due to limited workforce and existing workforce lack knowledge and intent to adapt to the technology available. As part of FCPA compliance, each visit/ requirement needs to be updated in the central ERP system, and the internet bandwidth available was just at 512 KBPS. This situation was handled by

1. Changing the hiring strategy: Fresh graduates were hired from Engineering colleges as they don't come with predefine blockage and have the commitment toward learning. Although identified such an individual was of challenge in itself

2. Focused and regular upskilling: Existing workforce were taught how to operate a laptop along with constant and rigorous training on ERP.

3. Breaking the "Sir' Culture: Most of the team members were not comfortable in calling out Superior's name and to tackle this cultural diversity Senior membership team held a regular meetup in order to bring in equality.

4. Promoting Open cabins policy: A strict mandate was issued to all the cabin holder that no one should turn away any teammate if he seeks support and similarly team members where encourage to walk in any time at cabins

This transaction was a big challenge, and people with B2B professional selling were in great demand. This broke the unspoken elite club of business groups and business professionals.

I was fortunate to be a professional resource, in-demand and joined the fortune 500 company as national sales head to get professional B2B selling implemented post the acquisition. Post joining after understanding the as – is situation and to do change management, requested HR team to align us with campus hiring. Started with a team of twenty-five Campus recruits on ground and Junior -Mid-Senior level management of legacy acquired companies.

The structured way of selling put in place at ground Graduate Trainees without baggage were bringing the change – Mid and Senior management due to the review process put in place by self had to align to the change.

While this process was in progress ensured to have ears to the ground and to do real handholding as a leader stayed, together in same guest house with my trainees for a period of 3 months and we developed the energy and enthusiasm to make this change happen with great amount of trust.

Though it was tough for few guys in mid-management to change and we had planned for such losses and could get fast learners in trainees who could help us manage the change and ensure its sustainability.

This way soon, we could reach a level wherein we complied to all global best practices and the global team as well-validated same with appointing an Expert as the MD for some period. This was truly a successful merger of Indian groups and customers and organisations along with employees gained with the value each created and enhanced.

The other is for a period of 2009 – 2011, wherein again global acquisitions were made on the basis of which sector is being in, an accelerated growth sector mode, post 26/11 in India. In one of the large fortune 500 expansion plan , one was made *on the basis of data analysis and analogy , that in Soft drink beverage US has X consumption per person and in India Y So analysing the data and keeping in mind the scope for growth in the Indian market the multinational company acquired local beverage companies and expanded its approach in the sunrise sector (Say Security/Life safety /Energy Efficiency/Transport. . Similarly, per capita basis if we analyse security per* person in US is X USD then on Indian population base it will be Z., and it will have room for growth and improvement.

The full strategy was based on analysis wetted by a leading M&A organisation, and the same was done with aggressive valuations. The realization was as well quite fast that however simple the math might seem, it's not working the same way, due to conditions on the ground. All Education and advocacy strategies as well didn't work to expand the market. This inorganic growth was planned more on the logic of bundling and setting right the business profitability issues. The Indian market and consumers were smart enough to understand and review offers with break down models. Package together like an aggregator was not making, value sense in B2B markets. The client feels after a point huge liability issue, as well, by going with one player. Along with same the ecosystem as well needs to get mature so that client, get options and can evaluate; what works in mature may not work in emerging markets as the desired ecosystem and the need may not exist.

Post-2010, this decade the M&A will be and has been across industries, as a traditional Organization & Technology Organization – Marriage. We have seen the same happening Walmart + Flipkart. The challenges here are Cultural, as both come with there own legacy and together need to create value for customers.

Initial M&A started with premise of expanding and globalization, and on selling side there was change which was from Managed Sales, as the market was small and there were few players in ecosystem,   to Professional selling, and now thanks to Digitization and Democratization of markets, it's learning of new Tech Tools and using Technology to create convenience for service and value with more choices and speed. The agenda in both stages, beings of growth and expansion. This method is one of the techniques & strategy to scale the business fast.

CHAPTER
Eight

India Market Uniqueness

The **economy of India** is one of the developing market economies, and is the world's 5th Largest economy by (GDP) Gross Domestic Product, (private consumption + gross investment + government investment +government spending +net exports) and the 3rd Largest by (PPP) Purchasing power parity. From independence since 15th Aug 1947 until 1991, successive governments promoted Protectionist economic policies with extensive government license Raj.; the end of the cold war in a global environment and an acute balance of payment crisis in 1991 led to the adoption of a broad liberalisation. Since the start of the 21st century, annual average GDP growth has been 6% to 7%, and from 2014 to 2018, India was the world's fastest-growing economy.

There are few uniqueness about Indian market one which has been there for the first two decades, and today most of the Global and local organization are thriving to address them:

Chaos: Most of the Global MNC fail to access market needs as they have a predefined portfolio and expects the market to accept the way it is. This attitude creates a challenge if you look from the customer's point of view since we expect more in terms of feature and customizability.

Unstructured: When compared to global markets, Indian markets are not structured in the way the US or Europe is, and this is primarily due to low product development and research. In most of the time, we have been in trial and testing mode itself as we operate in more me-too offering mode and being a potential market startup offering global me to a product have also flourished (e.g. OLA, Flipkart etc.). More of a Jugaad techniques or workable solutions.

Infrastructure: Its been an pain point for quite some time. We are still in developing face till date we lack basic need and look at government for aids. This is primarily due to the nature we operate, which results in global MNC restrain themselves for charting an aggressive growth plan in India.

Pricing: If you look at any global MNC's till today their entire growth strategy is around US Europe and China and primarily due to margins made in these market.

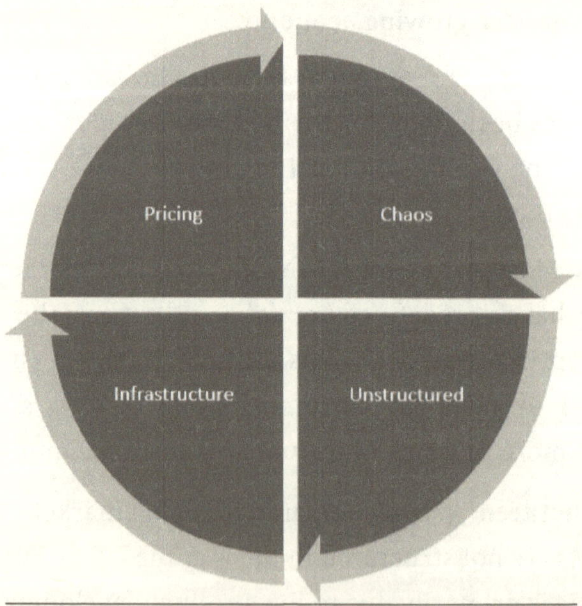

These market uniqueness confused most of the companies still wonder why on certain products margin and demand is good when compared to the overall sectoral performance, for example currently there is low demand in the overall Automobile sector in India. Most of the established brands are struggling to cope up with falling demand whereas on another side certain brand like MG hector are posted with excess booking, and also customers are willing to wait.

Also in recent years, reconciling the past with the present and the future has become a challenge. Developing mutual trust between the government and the public is vital in emerging India.

Half a century of planned economic development has culminated in rigid labour laws, fragmentation in industrial and agricultural sectors, and emphasis on inclusive growth with priority for the development of entrepreneurship, industrial units, and backward areas, supported by appropriate lending, concessions and subsidies, to bring about all-round growth. The economic structure followed that course, paving the way for further growth in the 'reforms' era since the 1990s.

India is an incredible country that presents many challenges and great opportunities. The local expertise is needed to unlock everything about today's Indian consumer. The Indian market has different markets within itself, starting from Urban to Rural and from Malls to Mela. We have trends affecting India and hone in on the regional differences, from socio-economic groups to demographics such as age, gender and household composition. We have Consumers in Metro and Tier 1 to 3 cities across the 4 main regions and in 6 local languages.

India 2020: 5 Sectors Driving The Country's Growth

- Infrastructure: Building A Place To Do Business, Working to Warehousing.

- Financial Services: The Mobile Path Toward Credit. ...E-Banking and E -Vallet.

- Technology: Leveraging A Massive Online Population. ..E verification to Aadhar.

- Automotive: Speeding Toward The Top Three. .. Transaction on move-Combustion to EV.

- Healthcare: Caring For An Aging Population... Insurance to Assisted living housing.

India is poised to become the third-largest **consumer market** behind only the US and China; and **consumer** spending in **India** is expected to grow from USD 1.5 trillion at present to nearly USD 6 trillion by 2030, a World Economic Forum report. We have USD 5 Trillion plan and mission by 2025 set by our transformational national leadership for India.

CHAPTER
Nine

VUCA Environment

VUCA is an acronym used by the American Military to describe extreme conditions in Afghanistan and Iraq. It stands for Volatile, Uncertain, Complex and Ambiguous. The deeper meaning of each element of VUCA serves to enhance the strategic significance of VUCA foresight and insight, as well as the behaviour of groups and individuals in organizations. It discusses systemic failures and behavioural failures, which are characteristic of organizational failure.

- **V** = Volatility: the nature and dynamics of change, and the nature and speed of change forces and change catalysts.

- **U** = Uncertainty: the lack of predictability, and the sense of awareness and understanding of issues and events.

- **C** = Complexity: the multiplex of forces, the confounding of issues, no cause-and-effect chain and confusion that surrounds organization.

- **A** = Ambiguity: the haziness of reality, the potential for misreads, and the mixed meanings of conditions; cause-and-effect confusion.

These elements present the context in which organizations view their current and future state. They come together in ways that either confound decisions or sharpen the capacity to look ahead, plan and move ahead. VUCA sets the stage for managing and leading.

The particular meaning and relevance of VUCA often relate to how people view the conditions under which they make decisions, plan forward, manage risks, foster change and solve problems. In general, the premises of VUCA tend to shape an organization's capacity to:

1. Anticipate the Issues that Shape

2. Understand the Consequences of Issues and Actions

3. Appreciate the Interdependence of Variables

4. Prepare for Alternative Realities and Challenges

5. Interpret and Address Relevant Opportunities

For most contemporary organizations – business, the military, education, government and others – VUCA is a practical code for awareness and readiness. Beyond the simple acronym is a body of knowledge that deals with learning models for VUCA preparedness, anticipation, evolution and intervention.

Anticipating change as a result of VUCA is one outcome of resilient leadership. The capacity of individuals and organizations to deal with VUCA can be measured with a number of engagement themes:

1. Knowledge Management and Sense-Making

2. Planning and Readiness Considerations

3. Process Management and Resource Systems

4. Functional Responsiveness and Impact Models

5. Recovery Systems and Forward Practices

6. Systemic failures

7. Behavioural failures

At some level, the capacity for VUCA management and leadership hinges on enterprise value systems, assumptions and natural goals. A "prepared and resolved" enterprise[4] is engaged with a strategic agenda that is aware of and empowered by VUCA forces.

complexity

Characteristics: The situation has many interconnected parts and variables. Some information is available or can be predicted, but the volume or nature of it can be overwhelming to process.

Example: You are doing business in many countries, all with unique regulatory environments, tariffs, and cultural values.

Approach: Restructure, bring on or develop specialists, and build up resources adequate to address the complexity.

volatility

Characteristics: The challenge is unexpected or unstable and may be of unknown duration, but it's not necessarily hard to understand; knowledge about it is often available.

Example: Prices fluctuate after a natural disaster takes a supplier off-line.

Approach: Build in slack and devote resources to preparedness—for instance, stockpile inventory or overbuy talent. These steps are typically expensive; your investment should match the risk.

ambiguity

Characteristics: Causal relationships are completely unclear. No precedents exist; you face "unknown unknowns."

Example: You decide to move into immature or emerging markets or to launch products outside your core competencies.

Approach: Experiment. Understanding cause and effect requires generating hypotheses and testing them. Design your experiments so that lessons learned can be broadly applied.

uncertainty

Characteristics: Despite a lack of other information, the event's basic cause and effect are known. Change is possible but not a given.

Example: A competitor's pending product launch muddies the future of the business and the market.

Approach: Invest in information—collect, interpret, and share it. This works best in conjunction with structural changes, such as adding information analysis networks, that can reduce ongoing uncertainty.

The capacity for VUCA leadership in strategic and operating terms depends on a well-developed mindset for gauging the technical, social, political, market and economic realities of the environment in which people work. Working with deeper smarts about the elements of VUCA may be a driver for survival and sustainability in an otherwise complicated world.

Psychometrics which measure fluid intelligence by tracking information processing when faced with unfamiliar, dynamic and vague data can predict cognitive performance in VUCA environments.

The solutions in VUCA world:

People determine the success of every Organization This requires the right framework conditions under which each individual can and may contribute his or her skills and services in the sense of agreed – more qualitative and quantitative – results. This was valid at all times and became even more critical in VUCA times. WHEREAS and HOW to determine the dialogue and discourse of managers and companies with their employees. The willingness to engage in genuine cooperation and take on clear responsibilities is an essential prerequisite for innovation. This requires freedom, creativity, speed, flexibility and a corporate culture that connects people with the organization. This connection becomes more significant and can be brought into the focus of leadership even more decisively. In a VUCA world, the most important thing is to anticipate the future and to strengthen cooperation in companies with modern solutions. Decisions and connections are success factors for shaping the common cause. The aim is to channel the energy used in any case into meaningful channels so that it can lead to value-adding approaches and measures.

VISION

Paint a picture of the future you want. Together; as a compass and for orientation; in order to confer meaning and spark motivation – and to forge an internal and external identity and effectiveness.

UNDERSTANDING

Understand interconnections; make them transparent. Reflect on the context. Think and plan meta-strategically. Start from the result and work backwards. Harmonise skills. Embrace and exploit behaviours and reactions. Convert anxiety and resistance to produce energy.

CLARITY

Simplicity. Focus on what counts and what it's really about. Trust, transparent connections and processes. Apply energy and force exactly where they will be most effective.

ADAPTABILITY / AGILITY

Flexibility. Agility. Scrutinise hierarchical management techniques. Promote a consistent culture for making decisions and accounting for mistakes. Interact transparently with objections. Facilitate innovation and build up resilience.

We can succeed despite uncertainty by staying relevant to all potential buyers at all times.

CHAPTER *Ten*

Technology – Industry 4.0 Enabler or Disruptor

I will cover in detail in our sequel, here just wanted to touch upon few points and brief you as in two decades post 1990...2010 was time when Technology had started disrupting the way business is done. In this chapter want introduce you to the concept of Industry 4.0 and in Sequel will cover how post-2010, the same needs to used in business for our advantage.

Industry 1.0: Refers to the first industrial revolution. It is marked by a transition from hand production methods to machines through the use of steam power and water power. The implementation of new technologies took a long time, so the period which this refers to it is between 1760 and 1820, or 1840 in Europe and the US. Its effects had consequences on textile manufacturing, which was first to adopt such changes, as well as iron industry, agriculture, and mining, although it also had societal effects with an ever stronger middle class. It also had an impact on British industry at the time.

Industry 2.0: The second industrial revolution or better known as the technological revolution is the period between 1870 and 1914. It was made possible with the extensive railroad networks and the telegraph which allowed for faster transfer of people and ideas. It was also marked by ever more present electricity which allowed for factory electrification and the modern production line. It was also a period of high economic growth, with an increase in productivity. It, however, caused a surge in unemployment since many workers were replaced by machines in factories.

Industry 3.0: The third industrial revolution occurred in the late 20th century, after the end of the two big wars, as a result of a slowdown with the industrialization and technological advancement compared to previous periods. It is also called the digital revolution/ IT Revolution or Software. The global crisis in 1929 was one of the adverse economic developments which had an appearance in many industrialized countries from the first two revolutions. The production of Z1 (electrically driven mechanical calculator) was the beginning of more advanced digital developments. This continued with the next significant progress in the development of communication technologies with the supercomputer. In this process, where there was extensive use of computer and communication technologies in the production process. Machines started to abrogate the need for human power in life.

Industry 4.0: The fourth industrial revolution is leading to the significant transformation, which is taking what we started in third with the adoption of computers, automation and enhance it with smart & autonomous system. "Industry 4.0" factories have machines which are augmented with wireless connectivity and sensors, connected to a system that can visualize the entire production line and make decisions on its own.

In essence, industry 4.0 is the trend towards automation and data exchange in manufacturing technologies and processes which include cyber-physical systems (CPS), the internet of things (IoT), industrial internet of things (IIOT), cloud computing, cognitive computing and artificial intelligence.

In Summary, the First Industrial Revolution used water and steam power to mechanize production. The Second used electric power to create mass production. The Third used electronics and information technology to automate production. Now a Fourth Industrial Revolution is building on the Third, the digital revolution that has been occurring since the middle of the last century. It is characterized by a fusion of technologies that is blurring the lines between the physical, digital, and biological spheres.

We are midst of this fourth industrial revolution, and the real determining factor is the pace of change. The correlation of the speed of technological development and, as a result, socio-economic and infrastructural transformations with human life allow us to state a qualitative leap in the rate of growth, which marks a transition to a new time era.

Major shifts on the demand side are also occurring, as growing transparency, consumer engagement, and new patterns of consumer behaviour (increasingly built upon access to mobile networks and data) force companies to adapt the way they design, market, and deliver products and services.

On the whole, there are four main effects that the Fourth Industrial Revolution has on business—on customer expectations, on product enhancement, on collaborative innovation, and on organizational forms. Whether consumers or businesses, customers are increasingly at the epicentre of the economy, which is all about improving how customers are served. Physical products and services, moreover, can now be enhanced with digital capabilities that increase their value. New technologies make assets more durable and resilient, while data and analytics are transforming how they are maintained. A world of customer experiences, data-based services, and asset performance through analytics, meanwhile, requires new forms of collaboration, particularly given the speed at which innovation and disruption are taking place.

New customer behaviour, ever-changing expectations of customers with the technological advancements are causing a significant shift in B2B sales.

Here are the four fundamental changes that the fourth industrial revolution has brought to sales:

Customer experience is key

More than 50% of the global population now uses social media platforms to connect, learn, and share information. This has given birth to digital selling, creating a digital (

always on, always available) experience for the customers. In an ideal world, these interactions would provide an opportunity for cross-cultural understanding and cohesion. However, they can also create and propagate unrealistic expectations as to what constitutes success for an individual or a group, as well as offer opportunities for extreme ideas and ideologies to spread. This is making interesting twists in the way we sell in the new digitalisation era 1

Apps and social media have created engagement, transparency and choice possible. We now have sophisticated customers who know exactly what they want and won't settle for less. Thus, sales success is constantly adapting to match a customer-driven market. Going forward into the Fourth Industrial Revolution customer experience needs to be the number one priority for any company. If you don't put customers at the top of your business, then you risk being lost in an ever-changing market.

Customers want to feel like they are number one and don't want to feel like just another number. They expect companies to understand their needs and bring the solutions that they want.

Technological advancement like analytics of customer behaviour, buying patterns, changing preferences are helping us to better understand the customer, with access to a wealth of information that will add a personal touch to their customer service. This is the key!

Cross-team collaboration

By putting the customer at the core of your sales strategy, it is essential to map out their journey. You need to join the customer where they are in their journey and help them get to the next level.

You will quickly realise that the customer will touch many departments. Thus, the Fourth Industrial Revolution will bring more collaboration within a company, with different departments working together to create a seamless customer experience.

By involving all departments in the sales strategy, and having them understand the customer, you will ensure that your customer service is more effective as the customers' needs will be known to all member of staff that they may connect with.

Embrace the change

The world is constantly evolving and changing. As Heraclitus once said, 'The only constant is change.' Every day new competitors will start disrupting the market, new tools will be developed, and market conditions change. To keep ahead of the market, always keep up to date with evolutions and don't be afraid of having to adapt.

Companies will always have to review their sales strategies to stay relevant and keep up with new disrupters. Be creative and find more ways for your brand to build a stronger connection with your business and how to improve your processes.

Advances in Sales Tools Technology

The link between sales strategies and technology has become more apparent over the past decade, to the point where sales teams rely on technology to carry out their job. By finding new sales technologies early, you will advance your company, and it will give you a real competitive advantage.

New technologies have become increasingly advanced. That they can now help determine the next moves and give recommendations for you to close deals. With the implementation of new technologies like Artificial Intelligence, it will turn the industry on its head, with the companies welcoming new technologies to come out on top.

The success of a company's sales strategy with the Fourth Industrial Revolution is all about the entire business coming together to exceed customer expectations. No matter how large or small your company is if your customer is not at the heart of every decision you make, you will eventually fail.

Fourth Industrial Revolution may indeed have the potential to "robotize" humanity and thus to deprive us of our heart and soul. No wonder you see robots who know precise specifications of the products and can talk to us in natural language. They can replace humans. But what really complements this is the best parts of human nature—creativity, empathy, stewardship. This is what really makes selling unique. It is incumbent on us all to make sure the latter prevails.

Stay tuned as more will be shared in the sequel of how these changes impacted business post-2010 and the decade to come.

*** Disclaimer, all names of organisations and people, are fictitious any resemblance is merely a coincidence.